F A Q

of the Christian Faith

by

r. j. arthur

under shepherd, teacher, author, lecturer, student

Published by the P.A.C. of America

F.A.Q. of the Christian Faith

ISBN: 978-1494744588

Printed in the United States of America

F A Q

of the Christian Faith

by

r. j. arthur
under shepherd, teacher, author, lecturer, student

_____
name

This book is dedicated to my Father

(and to all my family)

A Personal Note from the Author

The older I become, the more I value relationships. I suppose this may be a natural maturing process; however, along with this natural development, I hope I am also spiritually maturing. Natural maturity comes with time and experiences; spirituality comes through knowing and obeying God.[1] Even though I started my spiritual journey over twenty-six years ago, in some ways I am just now beginning to grow. The more I get to know and obey my heavenly Father through Jesus the Christ, the more I cherish our relationship.

Physical things in this world often reflect aspects of the spiritual. For instance, to those who have received Jesus the Christ, to those who believe in His name, God calls them His children. Having an earthly father, being a son, along with being a father to my own children, has given me a greater opportunity to understand what it means to have a spiritual relationship with a heavenly Father.

I have been blessed to have been raised in a loving home with a caring family. This has laid a valuable solid foundation that has allowed me to build much of my life. I do not want to be misunderstood or misrepresent the realities in my life. Relationships are hard and are not without challenges. My family relationships are not always the perfect 'leave it to beaver' ideal. My life lessons learned through my valued family ties have often come through the dysfunctions, drama, and hardships that come with having close relationships. Even in spite of the hardship, it would be unfortunate if an individual did not invest, in their earthly family. What an even greater tragedy if one never dedicates the time or disciplines to intimately know their heavenly Father and spiritual family.

This short book tells the story of how I began my spiritual journey. It describes where I was and how I began my relationship with my heavenly Father. I implore the present reader to invest the time to pursue an intimate personal relationship with their Creator. We are all in this spiritual journey together. I am just one beggar that desires to tell others where I found some bread.

r. j. arthur

How To Use This Study

The FAQ of the Christian Faith has seven sections that progressively teaches the good news, or the gospel, of the Christian faith. Each section, or lesson, contains the following:

- text that teaches various aspects of this good news
- an illustration summarizing the teaching of the session
- step by step instructions how to draw the illustration
- questions pertaining to the session

Each section or lesson is called a session. Theoretically, a student could complete a session in about twenty to thirty minutes. Since there are seven sessions, someone could read and complete this FAQ workbook within one week by completing one session per day. However, if the student desires to experience even greater benefits, they could study one session every day throughout the week. At this pace, it will take a student seven weeks to complete the FAQ of the Christian Faith. It is suggested that the student work through one session each week by completing the following:

- read through the same session every day for one week
- look up and read each of the scriptural footnotes within the session sometime throughout the week
- daily draw out the illustration while verbally communicating the message (this will allow the student to memorize the illustration and message)
- daily reflect upon and answer the questions pertaining to the session

Drawing the Session's Illustration

Drawing out each session is an important exercise that should not be overlooked. After reading the text of a session the student should examine the corresponding illustration. Following the illustration is a message with step by step instructions on how to draw out the illustration. The student should daily practice drawing the illustration on an 8½" by 11" piece of paper while verbally communicating the message (note: every time the student practices drawing out the illustration, the student should start with session one and finish with the current session's new additions). After the student is comfortable with drawing and communicating the illustration, the student should then draw the illustration in the diagram representing a blank piece of paper within their workbook. Knowing what to draw will remind the student what to say; and vice versa, knowing the message will remind the student what to draw. To effectively learn how to draw out the illustration, the student may initially want to have someone read the message while they draw out the illustration. Again, the goal is to be able to communicate the message while drawing it out.

To help the student memorize the message and illustration, the entire message with step by step instructions on how to draw the illustration is located at the end of this workbook. The student should regularly practice developing their skill until they feel comfortable to regularly present this illustration in order to make disciples of Christ.

How To Use This Study

Following each illustration is a series of questions pertaining to the text of that session. The student should begin answering and reflecting upon the questions after reading the text. The student can work on answering a question or two every day. Some students find it helpful to read the questions before reading through the text. When recording their answers, a student may find it helpful to record where they found the answer within the text (e.g. page 22, 2nd paragraph). The student may want to mark or highlight the text that provided the basis for their answer. The questions are designed to help in comprehending the main points of each session. The student will notice that the order of the questions directly correspond to the chronological order of the text in each session. For instance, question number one will deal with the first part of the text; question two will deal with the next part of the text; and so forth.

God has promised that His word will always do the work He intended. His word is powerful and presently active. There are all kinds of reasons why people may want to understand the basics of the Christian faith. For those who desire to know God, He will clearly reveal Himself through the truth of the Bible.

F A Q
of the Christian Faith

As we begin, I have two questions:

1). "What is the passion or purpose of your life?" (i.e. Why are you here? How do you wish to be remembered? What is the highest priority in your life?)

Answer #1:

2). "On a scale of one through ten (ten being the best), how well does the way you live your life reflect your priorities or purpose?"

Answer #2:   1   2   3   4   5   6   7   8   9   10
(circle honestly)

I would now like to share with you something someone once shared with me that helped me answer these two questions by explaining God's plan of redemption for Humanity.

Session 1: *Aspects of Sin*

In this session we consider three aspects of sin:
1). What is a sinner?
2). Where did sin come from?
3). What exactly is sin?

Most people would not consider it a compliment if they were called a sinner. In fact, people often use this word in a demeaning or derogatory manner. The Bible does not use this word in this kind of harsh demoralizing fashion. The Bible uses the term "sinner" to describe one's spiritual nature. Being a sinner simply means that someone has a sin nature; and by acting upon this nature they sin. It should be understood that one's nature is not produced by one's actions.[2] It is actually quite the opposite; one's nature produces one's actions. A person's actions actually identifies the origin of one's nature. When you sin, it is because you have a nature or propensity to sin. Rest assured, as a sinner, you are not alone. The Bible states that every single human that has ever lived is a sinner.[3] As previously stated, being a sinner simply means that you have a nature or propensity to sin; but where did you get this sin nature?

To answer the question concerning the origin of our sin nature, we need to go all the way back to the beginning of time. In the beginning there was a holy and just God. He has always been, and always will be, a holy and perfect God.[4] He created everything: the heavens and earth, the plants, all the animals, and He also created the first humans – Adam and Eve.[5] He formed Adam's body from the dust of the ground. Then God breathed the breath of life into Adam's nostrils and he became a living being.[6] God created Adam with both physical life and spiritual life. God is the creator and giver of life; His holy nature is the standard by which everything else is compared. At this time in history, all of God's creation, including human beings, possessed and reflected God's holy and perfect nature.[7]

In Genesis, the first book of the Bible, we also learn that God placed Adam in a special garden in a place called Eden so he could fulfill his created purpose.[8] This is the intended purpose of mankind: to glorify God by reflecting His nature through a perfect ideal relationship with God. In this garden where mankind could fulfill their intended purpose, there were all kinds of fruit trees. The tree of the knowledge of good and evil was in the middle of the garden. God instructed Adam, "You are free to eat from any tree in the garden; but you must not eat from the tree of the knowledge of good and evil, for when you eat of it you will surely die."[9] God provided for Adam's every need so Adam could reflect God's nature in his relationship with his Creator.[10]

God also created Eve with both a physical and spiritual life.[11] She apparently also received the same instructions about the forbidden fruit in the middle of the garden. A serpent (i.e. Satan) approached her and tried to convince her to eat the fruit from the tree of the knowledge of good and evil. The first four words the Devil said to humanity was, "Did God actually say..?" Satan, even to this very day, constantly tries to deceive, cause doubt, or have people question the legitimacy of God's word. Satan asked Eve, "Did God actually say, 'You shall not eat of any tree in the garden'?" Eve answered him, "We may eat fruit from the trees in the garden, but God did say, 'You must not eat fruit from the tree that is in the middle of the garden, and you must not touch it, or you will die.'"[12] Did you notice that Eve did not exactly quote or understand what God had said? This gave the serpent the foothold he needed in order to deceive and manipulate her.

Tragically, Satan was successful in deceiving Eve, convincing her that she misunderstood what God had said. She ate the fruit from the tree of the knowledge of good and evil. After Eve ate the forbidden fruit she also gave some to her husband who was with her, and he also ate.[13] When this happened, for the very first time, sin entered the world through Adam's act of disobeying God's Word.[14] All of God's creation, not just Adam and Eve, was affected. God's creation no longer perfectly reflected God's nature and character. It was now tainted by Adam's disobedience. The Creator's desired relationship with Adam was altered due to his disobedience, or what the Bible calls sin. Sin is simply missing the mark. This is any action that does not perfectly reflect the nature of God.[15] Adam and Eve become sinners and immediately acquired a sin nature. After they sinned, they sewed fig leaves together to cover themselves and then they hid from God.[16] Their actions had a direct effect on themselves, their relationship with God, as well as on all of creation.

In summary, sin is any thought, word, or deed that does not perfectly reflect the character or nature of God. This occurs anytime someone does not perfectly obey God's word.[17] The author or originator of sin is Satan. A sinner is a person who has the nature to sin; that is, they reflect the nature of Satan rather than the nature of God. Lucifer was the most beautiful angelic created being. The dilemma for Lucifer was that He had pride. He rejected God and wanted humanity to worship him instead of God.[18] He relied on himself instead of trusting in God. This caused the most beautiful angel to fall from his lofty prestigious position.[19] We commonly know this angel by the name of Satan, the Devil, the Adversary, ruler of this world, etc. Have you ever had pride? Have you ever wanted the praise of men? Have you ever rejected God? Have you ever relied on your abilities instead of trusting God? Of course you have! Because a sinner possesses the nature of Satan. As we will see in the next session, as a result of Adam's sin, every single person is a sinner.

The following diagram illustrates the summary of this session:

- The line drawn across the folded paper represents an eternal timeline. A holy and just God has no beginning and no end.

- The word "God" on the left side of the page represents the one true holy God of the Bible.

- The male stick figure on the right represents Adam.

- The female stick figure on the right represents Eve.

- The "P" above the stick figures represents their physical nature.

- The "S" above the stick figures represents their spiritual nature.

- The word "sin" represents the sin of Adam that affected all of creation.

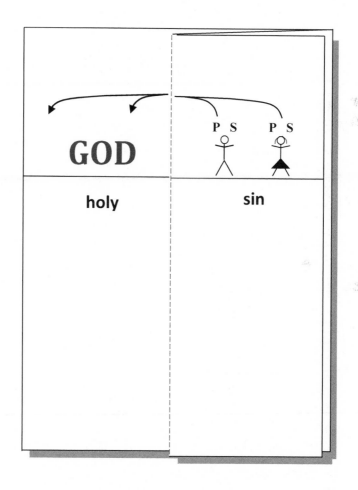

Drawing Session 1: *Aspects of Sin*

Message	Drawing
In the beginning there was, is, and always will be, a holy and just God.	*Draw a horizontal line about a third the way down. Write "**GOD**" above line on left. Write "**holy**" under line*
He created everything, including the first humans. God first created Adam with both physical life and spiritual life.	*Draw a man stick figure above line with "**P**" (physical) and "**S**" (spirit) above line on right*
God also created Adam's wife, Eve, with both physical and spiritual life.	*Draw a woman stick figure with "**P**" and "**S**" above*
God created mankind to have a personal relationship with God so they could serve and glorify Him.	*Draw lines and arrows to show God's purpose in creating mankind* 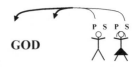

God instructed Adam, "You are free to eat from any tree in the garden; but you must not eat from the tree of the knowledge of good and evil, for when you eat of it you will surely die."

Tragically, Satan successfully convinced Eve to eat the fruit from the tree of the knowledge of good and evil. After Eve ate the forbidden fruit she also gave some to her husband Adam, who was with her, and he also ate. When this happened, sin entered the world through Adam's act of disobeying God's Word.

*Write "**sin**" under the stick figures*

1. Fold the right side of a piece of paper (preferably 8½" by 11") in half over the left side (letter "A" below).

2. Fold just the back half of the paper in half again (letter "B" below).

3. The paper should now look like letter "C" below.

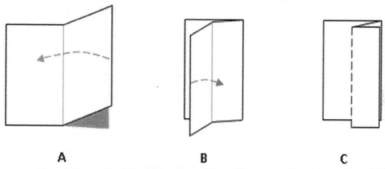

A   B   C

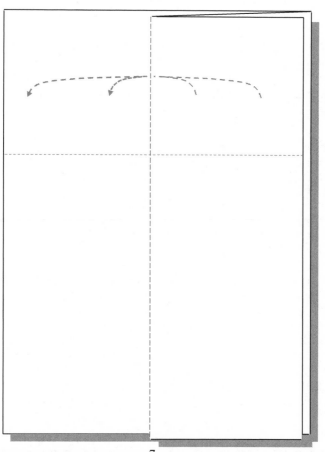

1.0 According to the Bible, how many people are sinners?

2.1 What is God's nature like?

2.2 Why did God create mankind (i.e. what is his intended purpose)?

3.1 What did God tell Adam that he was allowed to do?

3.2 What did God tell Adam that he was not allowed to do?

3.3 What did God tell Adam would happen if he did the very thing that God told him not to do?

3.4 What caused Eve to eat the fruit from the tree of knowledge of good and evil?

3.5 Who gave the forbidden fruit to Adam?

3.6 What did Adam and Eve do right after they disobeyed?

4.0 What is sin?

notes

Session 2: *Effects of Sin*

In this session we will explore three effects of Adam's disobedience:

1). What effect did Adam's disobedience have on the spiritual aspect of mankind?
2). What effect did Adam's disobedience have on the physical aspect of mankind?
3). What effect did Adam's disobedience personally have on you?

God had previously established the penalty for disobeying His word. The consequence of Adam's disobedience, or sin, was death.[20] Since God is a holy and just God, He is always true to His word. God, being true to His word, immediately imposed the penalty of death. God always keeps His word – this is part of His perfect and holy nature![21]

There are two kinds of death, each corresponding to the two aspects of man – physical death and spiritual death.[22] Death simply means separation. In physical death, the soul is separated from the physical body. Without the soul, the body ceases to function.[23] In spiritual death, the soul is separated from God (i.e. the source of life). As God promised, when Adam and Eve ate the fruit from the tree of knowledge of good and evil, Adam and Eve immediately spiritually died. This means they became spiritually dead; that is, separated from God! It was just as though a huge bottomless pit had opened between God and mankind. God is on one side and mankind completely spiritually isolated from God on the other. Man became sinful and therefore became separated from their holy Creator.

When Adam brought sin into the world by disobeying God's Word, Adam and Eve acquired a sin nature. Their thoughts, words, and actions became a reflection of their new spiritual father, Satan, instead of a reflection of their Creator God.[24] In essence, mankind became a prisoner or enslaved to sin.[25] The only choice they now possessed was to sin. Their sin nature is what now dictated their actions. When mankind acquired a sin nature, as God had promised, they died spiritually. Adam and Eve became slaves to sin and were no longer able to fulfill their intended purpose; which was, to glorify God through obedience within a perfect ideal intimate relationship with their Creator.

After Adam and Eve had sinned against God, they were ejected from the garden in Eden.[26] Not only did they immediately spiritually die, they began to physically die as well. Since God gave Adam responsibility over all of creation, all of creation was also affected by his sin. Things began to change. There was now pestilence, diseases, and eventually physical death.[27] Everything began to degenerate. This is evident even to this day. Are things improving? Is the gene pool getting more pure or more diluted? Are we acquiring more new species or are we losing species? It is estimated (depending on which science camp you follow) there are between 2000 up to 100,000 species going extinct every single year. The point is, when Adam and Eve sinned and sin entered all of creation, this not only had an immediate effect on their spiritual condition, but it altered all of the physical creation as well.

Adam and Eve lived what we might consider a 'normal' life. Though they were physically dying, they lived to be very old and had many children, who had many children, and so on. All the people from Adam and Eve to you and me have inherited some common human characteristics from Adam. We have ten fingers, ten toes, hair, two eyes, two ears, etc. Along with these characteristics, we also all inherited a human nature; the same type of nature as possessed by Adam. All of us were physically born into this world with a sin nature, which our "father" Adam acquired when he disobeyed God in the garden in Eden. This inherited sin nature has been passed on from one generation to the next. You might say, "It is in our jeans" (ha... ha.., an intentional pun on genes). It may also be noted that this sin nature is passed on from one generation to the next through the male.[28]

Since we all have inherited and entered this world with the same sin nature as Adam, we also enter the world spiritually separated from God as a slave to sin (i.e. spiritually dead). We have an everlasting soul but it is spiritually dead; that is, separated from God. Not only are we spiritually dead, we are also all physically dying. We are all in an environment that is self-destructive and degenerating. We have all inherited human characteristics, including a sin nature, but we cannot inherit spiritual life through our parents. We must receive spiritual life from God. Up to this point, things may seem very disheartening and grim. Keep reading... it eventually gets mind-blowingly better.

In Summary, the Bible says sin ultimately produces death (i.e. separation, destruction, degeneration, etc.). The following diagram illustrates the summary of this session:

- Putting an "X" through the "S" above each stick figure represents the spiritual death Adam and Eve immediately experienced when Adam disobeyed and sinned against God. This also represents the type of nature they now both possessed; that is, a sin nature.

- Opening up the folded piece of paper and drawing lines down each side, represents the spiritual separation that every human being experiences due to inheriting a sin nature from Adam.

- Writing "Physical Birth" on the top right side represents the only type of life that can be produced by humanity. We can only pass on physical life but we cannot give spiritual life.

- Drawing additional stick figures below the original two stick figures, represents the all the generations from Adam and Eve to you and me. Notice that all these generations are born with physical life, but none of them can be born with spiritual life. All the generations from Adam and Eve to you and me have been born spiritually separated from God.

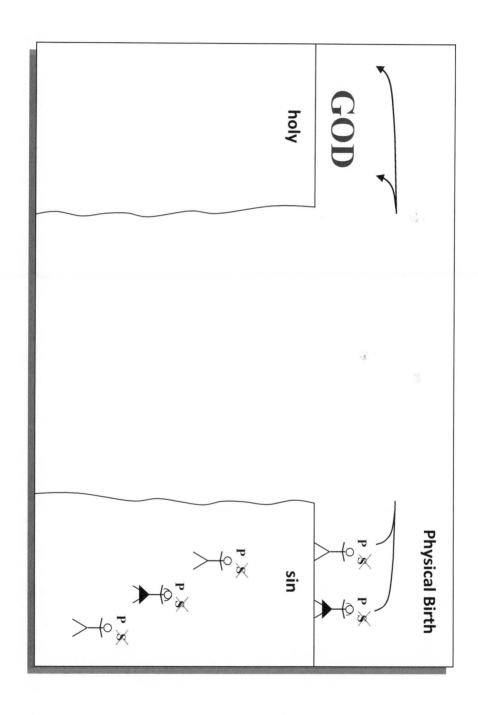

Session 2: *Effects of Sin*

Message	Drawing

Message

When mankind disobeyed God's word, they immediately died spiritually; meaning, they became separated from God!

It was just as though a huge bottomless pit had opened between God and mankind's relationship. Mankind became sinful and therefore became separated from God. When Adam brought sin into the world by disobeying God's word, he inherited a sin nature; and in fact, mankind became enslaved by sin.

Adam and Eve lived what we might consider to be a 'normal' life. Adam and Eve physically lived to be very old and had many children, who had many children, and so on. All the people from Adam and Eve to you and me were physically born into this world with a nature to sin, which has been inherited from Adam from one generation to the next.

Since we all enter this world with the same sin nature as Adam, we also enter the world spiritually separated from God (i.e. spiritually dead) as a slave to sin.

Drawing

Place an "X" (spiritual death) through the "S" located above stick figures:

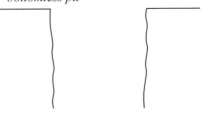

Open your paper as far as possible and draw the walls of the bottomless pit

Draw the additional stick figures under the other stick figures

Write "P" above the additional stick figures (physical life)

Write "S" with an "X" through it above each additional stick figure (spiritual death)

*Write "**Physical Birth**" in the top right hand corner of the paper*

14

1.0 What immediately happened when Adam and Eve disobeyed God's word (i.e. sinned)?

2.1 What does it mean to die physically?

2.2 What does it mean to die spiritually

3.0 After Adam sinned, what nature did Adam and Eve inherit?

4.0 What are some consequences due to Adam disobeying God's word (i.e. sinning)?

5.0 When parents have a sin nature, what kind of nature will their children inherit?

6.0 True or False. When an innocent little baby is physically born, they are born spiritually dead as a sinner; that is, spiritually separated from God.

notes

In this session we will explore:

1). How does humanity try to get to God?
2). Four common examples humans use to try to obtain spiritual life.

There are several ways that humanity tries to restore their broken relationship with God. People often try to get to God through their own efforts by building what we will call "human bridges." The sin nature naturally causes us to create and do things on our own instead of relying and trusting in God. We will even try to accomplish spirituality through our carnal ability which is motivated by our sin nature. It is a common misconception that if we try to do spiritual things then we will become spiritual. Or if we try to look and act spiritual then we will become spiritual. This makes perfect sense according to our sin nature, but it is not consistent with God's nature. To clarify this point, let's consider some common "bridges" people often attempt to build.

One of the bridges people try to build is "Good Works." People often believe if they do things that appear to be God-like or good, then they will be accepted by God. People commonly believe that if they do more good things than bad, then God will reward the good and forget about or overlook the bad. Unfortunately, God is not impressed with our good works. In fact, the Bible says our good deeds are as impressive to God as a pile of filthy disgusting used dirty rags.[29] All goodness has its origin with God, not with sinful man. Our attempts of acting good fall far short of spanning the chasm of our spiritual separation from God. Good works cannot deliver us from spiritual death over to spiritual life.

"Prayer" is another bridge people often rely on to spiritually reunite them to God. Many people believe that they must sincerely ask God to forgive their sins or say some kind of prayer for their relationship with God to be restored. It is almost if God were viewed as a genie in a magic bottle. If we ask God, then God will hop to and grant our request. Prayer is a way in which someone who has a restored relationship with God can communicate with their Creator; however, there is not any prayer that will restore a broken relationship, or bridge the gap, between mankind and God.

There are many people sitting in the pews of prominent, and not so prominent, churches that are trusting in church membership and/or attending "Church Gatherings" to bridge the gap between God and mankind. The Bible teaches that everyone who has had their relationship with God restored belong or are a part of the true church known as the ecclesia (i.e. called out ones). This is a spiritual group that God assembles, not a physical group that regularly has meetings. There is no group or regular assembly of people we can join that will restore our broken relationship with God. "Going to church" cannot reconcile man to God.

Although there are many bridges people attempt to build to try and reach God, for purposes of this illustration, the last bridge we will consider is the "Baptism" bridge. The word baptize is a transliterated word from the Koiné Greek language. The word simply means to be so immersed or saturated with something that you are identified with it. For instance, someone can be baptized in fear; meaning, they are so full of fear that if you look at them you would recognize that they are scared to death. Or someone could be baptized in love. We have all seen those couples that are oozing with love as they gaze into each other's eyes (Oh, yuck). Usually people reference baptism with being immersed or saturated with water. If one is relying on this baptism to bridge their relationship with God, they are simply all wet. Baptism with water can never restore one's relationship with God.

Though all these bridges fall far short in bridging the relational gap between mankind and God, it must be made perfectly clear that each of the so called bridges we discussed can have a very important place in our spiritual life. Spiritual actions flow out of spiritual people. But simply doing spiritual actions does not make someone spiritual. Humans put value on the outward actions, but God looks on the heart.[30] The dilemma for mankind is the heart. We need God to give us a new heart (i.e. new nature), and then spiritual actions will flow out of that new nature. No bridge humanity tries to build has the ability to give spiritual life! It is only after someone has been given spiritual life that spiritual actions can fulfill their designed purpose.

In summary, it is human nature to try and do things to reconcile the broken relationship between God and mankind. There are all kinds of religions and spiritual activities that mankind practices in order to try to become more spiritual. No action mankind does can bridge the relational gap between man and God.

The following diagram illustrates the summary of this session:

- The first platform or "bridge" is "Good Works." As can be seen in the illustration, the bridge of good works falls far short of bridging the gap between mankind and God.

- The next bridge is "Prayer." Simply asking, begging, or talking to God can never restore one's broken spiritual relationship to God. Individuals need a new heart. Putting one's hope in prayer is not the way to gain a new heart or nature.

- The next bridge is "Church Gatherings." Many well intended people put an emphasis on going to an event they call "church" or joining an exclusive "membership." From Genesis through Revelation, the Bible records man's failed attempts to please or gain access to God through various organized events.

- Though there are many spiritual things people try to do to please God in order to restore their broken relationship, for our purposes the last bridge is "Baptism." Again, many well intended people have trusted that they have a healthy relationship with God because they were immersed or saturated with water. There is no amount of water that can restore the broken spiritual relationship between humanity and God.

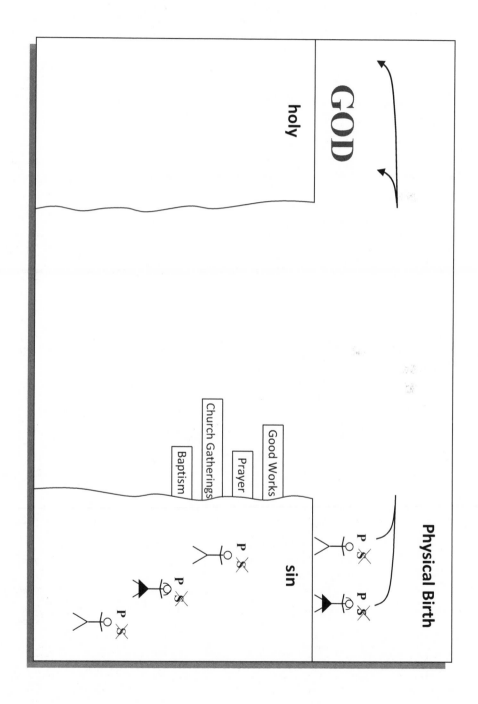

Drawing Session 3: *Human Methods*

Message	**Drawing**

People often try and restore their relationship with God through their own efforts. We will call these human efforts "bridges."

One of the bridges people try to build is called "Good Works." People often believe if they do more good things than bad, then God will give us the benefit of the doubt and overlook our bad. This is not so.

"Prayer" is another bridge people often rely on to spiritually reunite them to God. Many people believe that they must sincerely ask God to forgive their sins or say some kind of prayer for their relationship with God to be restored. This is not so.

There are many people trusting in church membership and/or attending "Church Gatherings" to bridge the gap between God and man. This will never work.

For purposes of this illustration, the last bridge we will consider is the "Baptism" bridge. If one is relying on baptism to bridge their relationship with God, they are simply all wet.

Though all these bridges fall far short in bridging the gap between man and God, each of these so called bridges can have an important place in one's spiritual life.

Questions for Session 3: *Human Methods*

1.0   **True** or **False. If someone desires to be spiritual then they must look and act spiritual.**

2.0   **Compared to the goodness of God, what does the bible say our good works (i.e. good deeds) are like?**

3.0   **True** or **False. In order for people to restore their broken relationship with God, they must earnestly pray for God to forgive them of their sins.**

4.0   **What is the true church here on earth?**

5.0   **What does the word "baptize" mean?**

6.0   **True** or **False. There is no spiritual value in doing spiritual things.**

notes

In this session we will explore:

    1). Does God exist?

    2). What is the definition of a false god?

    3). What are the consequences of trusting in false gods?

      Before someone could even try to have their spiritual relationship reconciled to God, one must acknowledge and understand the reality or existence of God. The Bible never tries to prove God's existence. The Bible simply states the fact, "In the beginning **GOD** created..." The Bible also states that God has clearly shown His eternal power and divine nature through creation; but, mankind will often not even acknowledge Him as their Creator or honor Him as God. People all too often turn their hearts away from God instead of pursuing a relationship with Him. The Bible says that God clearly shows His invisible attributes through creation; namely, his eternal power and divine nature. Therefore men are without any excuses because they should have known better, even if for no other reason, because creation reveals the evidence of God.[31]

      A friend recently told me an interesting story: There were two close friends that took very different paths in their youth. One became a devout believer in God, and the other an atheist. The atheist would claim that there is no evidence of God while the believer proclaimed that, at the very least, creation demonstrates the existence of God. The atheist became a devoted scientist who specialized in astronomy and said all of creation appeared by chance happenings. For his birthday, the believer had one of his engineering friends design and build a very precise working scale model of our solar system. All the planets were rotating at just the right speeds as they orbited the sun in their exact elliptical paths and velocities. The atheist was delighted with his gift. As he explored this replica of the universe, he was amazed at the accuracy and precision of the scale model. In complete astonishment the atheist asked, "Who was the engineer who designed and created this beautiful scale model. His Christian friend simply replied, "No one, it just appeared by chance over billions of years. I simply discovered it and gave it to you." God is a revealing Creator who can be seen and known. He is mindful, purposeful, and personally active with all of His creation.

As long as we are separated from God, our human devices and attempts to reach Him will be to no avail. Realizing that there is a God is perhaps the first step in pursuing reconciliation. It is only after someone comes to the realization that a personal revealing Creator actually exists, that they can pursue getting to know Him. Unfortunately, even after this realization, people will often be led astray by creating faulty systems or religions. These faulty systems or religions becomes their false faith in a false god. This is the god in which they are trusting. In fact, everyone has faith in something whether or not they believe in the one true God. Even the atheist has faith that there is no true faith. Our present culture is plagued with relativism. The only absolute truth that the relative thinker adopts is that there is absolutely no such thing as absolute truth. And they are absolutely sure that there is no absolute truth. Since there is only one true God, then there is only one true faith. Everyone has a god. Whatever or whomever people are trusting or believing in for their spiritual well-being, apart from the one true God, is their false god.

The tragedy is that when one's physical life on this earth comes to an end, and if they are still separated from God (i.e. spiritually dead) because of having trusted in erroneous ways of restoring their relationship with God, they will remain in that state forever. They will be separated from God forever in a place often referred to as hell (i.e. hades, the second death, lake of fire, etc.). The Bible calls this the second death because it is not the first death. The first death is the physical death, whereas the second death references spiritual death. And do you know how the Bible describes spiritual death? The second death is the complete separation from God in total darkness and isolation, under perpetual judgment and torment, without hope, forever and ever and ever![32] It is impossible for anyone to even begin to imagine how utterly horrible it is to be completely and permanently separated from God. Nor can words describe the misery that will be experienced by mind, soul, and body. Imagine spending forever in such a place apart from God. And the saddest reality is that this is totally unnecessary!

It is not God's desire that any person should be separated from Him in such a place.[33] It is His desire that every person would cross the chasm of separation and be united with Him in a perfect restored eternal relationship. God desires that every person should have spiritual life and spend eternity in a perfect relationship with Him. Because of His immeasurable love for us, His great mercy and amazing grace, God has provided a way for us to cross the great chasm separating mankind from God. God was under no obligation to do this. It is only out of His loving nature that God has provided a way for our relationship to be perfectly restored.[34]

In summary, there is only one true God and therefore only one absolute truth and only one true faith. God's existence is evident through creation. No one has any excuses for denying the existence of God. No one has any excuse for not pursuing a relationship with their Creator. The Bible says, "The fool says in his heart, 'There is no God.' They are corrupt, they do abominable deeds, there is none who does good."[35] In actuality, whether they realize it or not, whatever people are trusting in is their god. This could be science, one's own intellect, materialism, false religions, the bridges in our diagram, etc. There are eternal consequences in having faith in anything or anyone other than the one true God. If someone experiences the first death without having true faith in the one true God, they will experience the second death (i.e. spiritual death).

The following diagram illustrates the summary of this session:

- All the arrows going down from the "bridges" represent people having faith in false gods when they die.

- Writing the word "Hell" at the end of these arrows represents the second death (i.e. spiritual death).

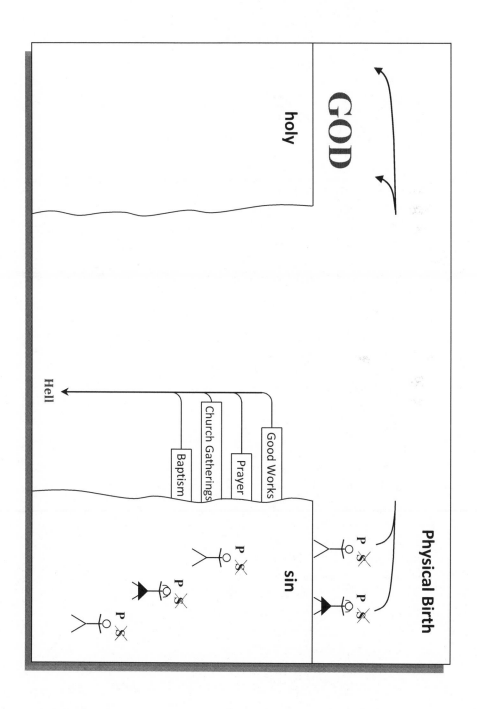

Drawing Session 4: *Trusting False gods*

| **Message** | **Drawing** |

As long as we are separated from God, our human devices and attempts to reach Him will be to no avail.

The tragedy is that when one's physical life on this earth comes to an end, and if they are still separated from God (i.e. spiritually dead) because of having trusted in erroneous ways of restoring their relationship with God, they will remain in that state forever. They will be separated from God forever in a place often referred to as hell (i.e. hades, the second death, lake of fire, etc.). The Bible calls this the second death because it is not the first death.

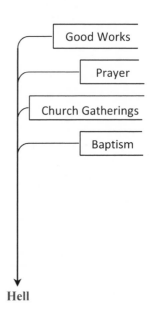

And do you know how the Bible describes spiritual death? The second death is the complete separation from God in total darkness and isolation, under perpetual judgment and torment, without hope, forever and ever and ever! It is impossible for anyone to even begin to imagine how utterly horrible it is to be completely and permanently separated from God. Nor can words describe the misery that will be experienced by mind, soul, and body.

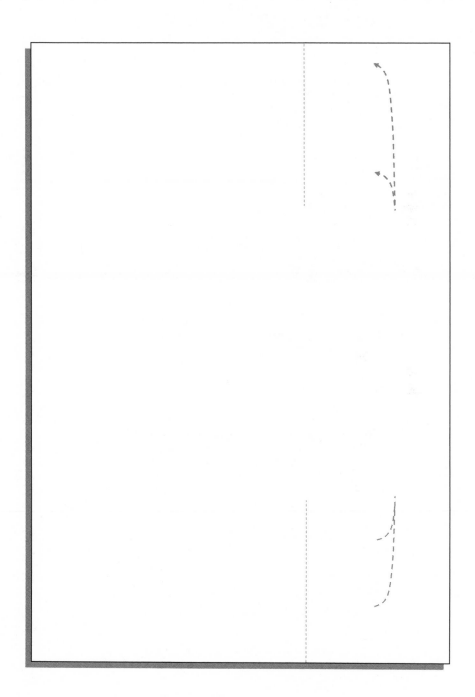

1.0   **What is at least one thing that clearly shows God's invisible attributes; namely, his eternal power and divine nature (Romans 1:18-20)?**

2.0   **True or False. Everyone believes in something (i.e. small "g" god).**

3.0   **True or False. Since there is only one true God, there is only one absolute truth and only one true faith.**

4.0   **Describe the first death and the second death.**

5.0   **What does God desire concerning a relationship with mankind?**

6.0   **According to the Bible, what does the fool say in his heart and how is a fool described (Psalm 14:1)?**

notes

_____

_____

_____

_____

_____

_____

_____

_____

_____

_____

_____

_____

_____

_____

_____

_____

_____

_____

_____

_____

_____

_____

_____

_____

_____

In this session we will explore:
1). What is the way to God, the truth of God, and the life of God?
2). What has Jesus done in order to bridge the gap between mankind and God?
3). Why would such a good man like Jesus die for a sinner like you and me?

Do you know the way to God? Jesus the Christ said, "I am the way, and the truth, and the life. No one comes to the Father except through me."[36] Jesus did not say that good works, prayer, church gatherings, baptism, or anything else is the way. He said: "I am the way." God the Son was sent by God the Father into this world to become 'The Bridge' between mankind and God. He is the only way by which we can cross the spiritual void created by sin. Sin produces spiritual death but God's love through Jesus the Christ produces spiritual life. "For God so loved the world, that he gave his only Son, that whoever believes in him should not perish but have eternal life."[37] By believing/trusting in Jesus as the only way, one will not experience spiritual death but will be given eternal life.

Not only did Jesus say He is the only way, Jesus also stated that there are no exceptions. He said that no one can come to God except through Him. There are no exceptions! Some people might think this is not fair, but this is the reality. Accepting or trusting in anything but Jesus will lead to the second death. This is the truth. Jesus said He is the way and the truth. There is only one Jesus and there is only one truth. Knowing the truth will set a person free.[38] The truth will free the individual who is enslaved by sin through their sin nature. Jesus the Christ is the way and the truth.

Jesus also said He is the life. Trusting in Him alone will give spiritual life. Through faith in Christ, an individual will cross over from spiritual death to spiritual life. And Jesus does not give just any kind of life; he gives eternal life. Eternal life is not just simply referring to the longevity of life, but the quality of life.[39] The spiritual life obtained through faith in Jesus is like no other. Christ gives an abundant life of the highest quality.[40] It is infinite, beyond description, provides peace that surpasses all understanding; it is eternal life. Jesus is the way, the truth, and the life.

What did Jesus the Christ actually do to become the bridge that reconciles mankind's relationship with God? Before answering that question, let's first review two basic points: 1) The penalty God established for sin is death (both physical and spiritual death); 2) Everyone is a sinner due to the fact that they have inherited a sin nature from their father. This is why it is a very important to understand that Jesus was born of a virgin.[41] He did not receive a sin nature like the rest of us. Jesus' nature has the same nature as His Father, who is God Himself. Since Jesus is like God and has no sin, He did not deserve the penalty of sin which is death. Since He did not have to die in order to pay the penalty for His own sin, Jesus could die in order to pay the penalty that we have earned because of our sin. If Jesus had a sin nature, this would not be an option because He would have to die to pay the penalty for His own sinfulness. By shedding His blood and dying upon the cross, being buried in the grave, and resurrected the third day according to the scriptures, Jesus became the life-giving savior for a sinful human race.[42]

God the Son (i.e. Jesus the Christ) is always in perfect harmonious fellowship with God the Father.[43] His entire existence is purposed to obey the Father in order to reveal the Father for the Father's glory. Glorifying God the Father is the core essence of Jesus' Personhood.[44] Though the physical agony of enduring an execution by means of crucifixion was horrific, there was something far worse Jesus had to endure. He even pleaded with the Father to not ask him to go to the cross.[45] Again, it was not just the physical pain that caused Jesus' greatest dread (though I am sure he wasn't looking forward to the physical agony of the crucifixion). Jesus did not want to even entertain the thought of being separated from His Father (i.e. both physical and spiritual death). None the less, Jesus submitted His own will to obediently do the will of the Father. He went to the cross and experienced the full wrath of God in order to pay for the sin of the world.[46] Jesus experienced the full brunt of the second death multiplied by the number of people in the world. Wow! Jesus was obedient, even to the point of dying on the cross, in order to glorify God.[47]

I am continually amazed that the Father would have Jesus the Christ die for me. I can maybe understand if someone were to sacrifice their life for a good or important person, but to give their life for a sinner who did not even know or acknowledge God? Even though I am completely wretched and Jesus is absolutely perfect, He still willingly gave his life.[48] Jesus the Christ is God Himself who became flesh by being born in the likeness of man.[49] He was born of a virgin.[50] He did not have a sin nature; but rather, He has the nature of His heavenly Father (i.e. God). The Bible describes God's perfection as righteous and every sinner is unrighteous. Christ is righteous (i.e. without sin) and therefore did not deserve to die, but He died in our place (i.e. the unrighteous). "For Christ also suffered once for sins, the righteous for the unrighteous, that he might bring us to God."[51] For one will scarcely die for a righteous person—though perhaps for a good person one would dare to die— but God shows his love for us in that while we were still sinners, Christ died for us.[52]

In summary, Jesus is the way, the truth, and the life. No one comes to God the Father apart from Him. The following diagram illustrates the summary of this session:

- The cross with Jesus the Christ written in the middle represents that Jesus is the way, the truth, and the life. He is The Bridge that God the Father has provided so mankind can cross over from spiritual death to spiritual life.

- John 14:6.

- John 3:16.

- 1 Peter 3:18a.

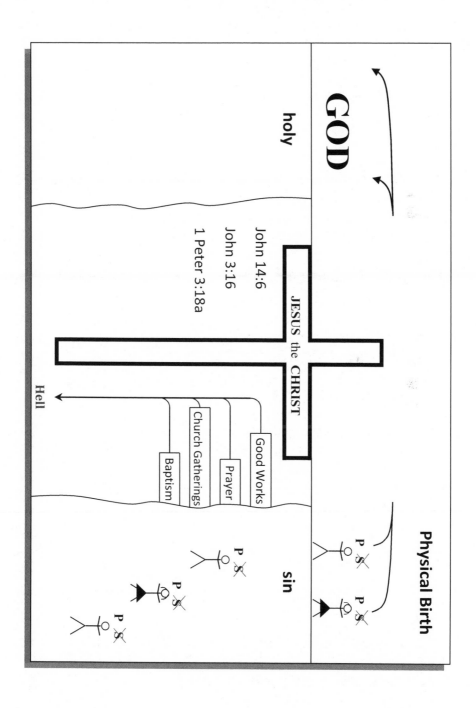

Drawing Session 5: *The Way to God*

Message	**Drawing**
Jesus said, "I am the way, and the truth, and the life. No one comes to the Father except through me."	Write "**John 14:6**" on the left side of the chasm.
"For God so loved the world, that he gave his only Son, that whoever believes in him should not perish but have eternal life."	Write "**John 3:16**" under "John 14:6"
Jesus is the way, the truth, and the life. What did Jesus Christ actually do to become this bridge? By shedding His blood and dying upon the cross, being buried in the grave, and resurrected the third day according to the Scriptures, Jesus became the life-giving savior that bridged the relational gap between all of mankind and God.	Draw the cross and write "**JESUS** the **CHRIST**" inside.

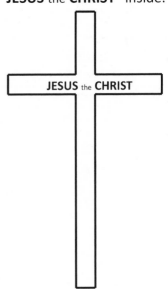

"For Christ also suffered once for sins, the righteous for the unrighteous, that he might bring us to God…"	Write "**1 Peter 3:18a**" under "John 3:16"

Questions for Session 5: *The Way to God*

1.0 **What did Jesus say was the way to God, the truth about God, and true spiritual life (i.e. John 14:6)?**

2.1 **What did Jesus actually do in order to become the bridge so that we can cross over from spiritual death to spiritual life?**

2.2 **Why would Jesus do this?**

3.0 **Look up in the Bible and write out the verse John 14:6.**

4.0 **Look up in the Bible and write out the verse John 3:16.**

5.0 **Look up in the Bible and write out the verse 1 Peter 3:18.**

notes

In this session we will explore:
1). What does it mean to be born again?
2). How does someone become a child of God?
3). What is the Tri-unity of God?

When we come to God by having faith in Jesus the Christ, we pass from spiritual death to spiritual life. When we receive Jesus through faith, God gives us spiritual life.[53] By receiving Jesus through faith, we are given eternal life that will never be taken away. One of the passages in the Bible that speaks of having this life by having Jesus is 1 John 5:11 and 12, "And this is the testimony, that God gave us eternal life, and this life is in his Son. Whoever has the Son has life; whoever does not have the Son of God does not have life."

In John 3:1-10, the Bible tells us about a man named Nicodemous who came to Jesus to make inquiries. Jesus explained to Nicodemous what must happen for him to cross the spiritual gap and enter the spiritual realm (i.e. God's kingdom). Jesus said, "no one can enter the kingdom of God unless he is born again." Being born again is referencing a second birth. Nicodemous said to Jesus, "How can a man be born when he is old? Can he enter a second time into his mother's womb and be born?" Nicodemous correctly understood the first birth as the physical birth into this physical world, but he was confused because he did not understand that the second birth Jesus was talking about is the spiritual birth into the spiritual world. Everyone who is physically born is born spiritually dead. Our physical parents give physical life but we need a spiritual parent (i.e. God) to give us spiritual life through a spiritual birth. The Bible says that one is born again and becomes a new creation through faith.[54] Just like with the physical birth, when someone is spiritually born through faith, they are born as a spiritual baby.

There was another man named John the Baptist that came to prepare for the coming of Jesus.[55] He baptized people in water as he proclaimed, "Repent, for the kingdom of heaven is at hand."[56] Repentance means to have a changed mind. Through the new birth, we get a new heart and changed mind.[57] John the Baptist said he was only baptizing with water, but Jesus baptizes people with the Holy Spirit.[58] Jesus totally immerses, or saturates, people with the Holy Spirit; meaning, they are identified with the Holy Spirit. At the moment someone believes with true biblical faith, they are born again. Upon regeneration (i.e. becoming a new creation), at that very moment, several things simultaneously happen: Jesus baptizes them with the Holy Spirit; they become a child of God; God becomes their spiritual Father; they receive a new nature with a new heart; they receive a new nature with a new mind; etc. The Holy Spirit is directly involved in this new birth process.[59]

Who is the Holy Spirit? Just like the Father is God, and Jesus the Son is God, so the Holy Spirit is God; and just like the Father is a Person, and Jesus is a Person, so the Holy Spirit is also a Person. The Spirit is not simply an active force or an it; He is a distinct Person of God. He has a personality, will, intellect, emotion, self-awareness; that is, He is a free moral agent. Christ did not teach there are three Gods; by no means, He clearly taught there is only ONE true GOD.[60] But Jesus clearly revealed that the one true God is God the Father; God the Son; and God the Holy Spirit; three Persons eternally coexisting in the Godhead, yet only one true God. Each Person is the exact same in substance, yet distinct in subsistence. This teaching is often known as the Trinity.[61] This is a difficult concept that can only be truly understood and accepted through faith by those that are born again (i.e. regenerate). Jesus gave His followers a command, which creates a symbolic picture of the tri-unity of God (i.e. Trinity).

One of the great missions, or things Jesus was to accomplish, was to reveal God's name. At the end of Jesus' incarnate ministry, He said to His Father that He had accomplished all that the Father had sent Him to do. He said that He had perfectly accomplished His mission of revealing God's name.[62] To reveal someone's name is to reveal the very essence or complete identity of that person. After Jesus was resurrected from the dead, right before He ascended up into heaven, He commanded His followers to go and help others know and follow His teachings (a follower of Jesus' teachings is called a disciple).[63] He commanded His disciples to go and make other disciples. One of the things the disciples were commanded to do was to immerse disciples into God's name. They were to immerse them into the Father, and immerse them into the Son, and immerse them into the Holy Spirit.[64] Water baptism symbolically shows that a disciple is identified with each Person by dipping someone into water three times. One dip for the Father; one dip for the Son; and one dip for the Holy Spirit. Three dips yet only one baptism into the name of God. This symbolic water baptism is a picture of a true believer being saturated and identified with the one true God; namely, God the Father, God the Son, and God the Holy Spirit. There are three dips yet only one baptism, just like there are three Persons yet only one true God.

When we are born again through faith in Christ, we become what the Bible calls a child of God. This new spiritual relationship is described in John 1:12-13, "But to all who did receive him, who believed in his name, he gave the right to become children of God, who were born, not of blood nor of the will of the flesh nor of the will of man, but of God." To be born again, to become a child of God, someone must receive Jesus and believe in His name. Again, when someone has faith (i.e. trusts, believes, etc.) in Jesus they receive Him. To believe in His name is to believe in the very essence, the true complete identity, of His very being.

What a great gift God has given us – to be part of His family. Through faith in Jesus the Christ, we become God's child and experience all the benefits of being a child of the Creator of the universe. Equally amazing is the fact that this newfound relationship with God is not something that will eventually happen. It is a now thing! We are born again and given eternal life at the very moment we believe and receive Christ through faith. We are a new creation and receive a new nature; the nature of our heavenly Father. Though a child of God also still has their old sin nature, lives are changed the moment they come to God through Christ as they receive God's nature.[65] Is it any wonder life takes on a new wonderful meaning? Is it any wonder we want to get to know God through the Bible or share the "Good News" of Jesus the Christ with others?

The following diagram illustrates the summary of this session: the "Spiritual Birth" at the top left; the people who crossed over The Bridge (i.e. who were born again) are spiritually alive (i.e. no "X" through the "S"); the "Born Again (John 3:1-10)" above the line showing people crossing over the bridge; and the additional verses "1 John 5:11-12 and John 1:12-13."

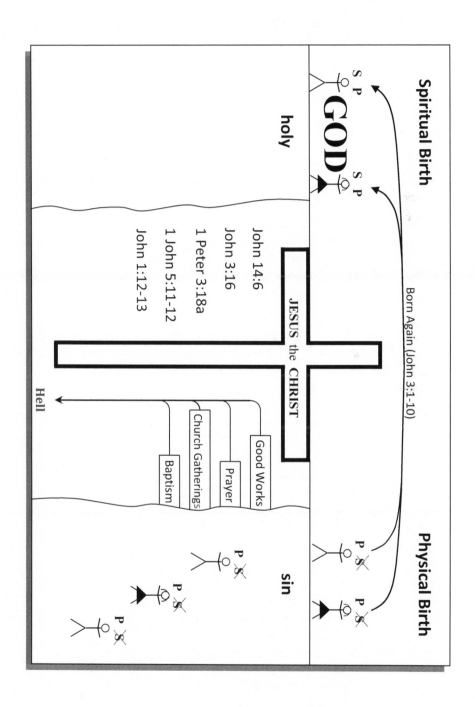

Drawing Session 6: *Being Born Again*

Message

Drawing

When we come to God by having faith in Jesus Christ, we pass from spiritual death to spiritual life.

Draw two new stick figures on the other side of the chasm, one on each side next to God. Write an "**S**" for spiritual life and a "**P**" for physical life above each stick figure.

S P   S P

To cross over from death to life, someone must receive Jesus and believe in His name. When someone has faith (i.e. trusts, believes, etc.) in Jesus they receive Him. To believe in His name is to believe in the very essence, the true complete identity, of His very being.

Draw an arrow from each stick figure on the "Physical Birth" side over to the "Spiritual Birth" side.

Write "**Spiritual Birth**" in the upper left-hand corner.

"And this is the testimony, that God gave us eternal life, and this life is in his Son. Whoever has the Son has life; whoever does not have the Son of God does not have life."

Write "**1 John 5:11-12**" under "1 Peter 3:18a."

When we are born again, we become what the Bible calls a child of God. "But to all who did receive him, who believed in his name, he gave the right to become children of God, who were born, not of blood nor of the will of the flesh nor of the will of man, but of God."

Write "**Born Again (John 3:1-10)**" on top of the line connecting the stick figures.

Write "**John 1:12-13**" under "1 John 5:11-12."

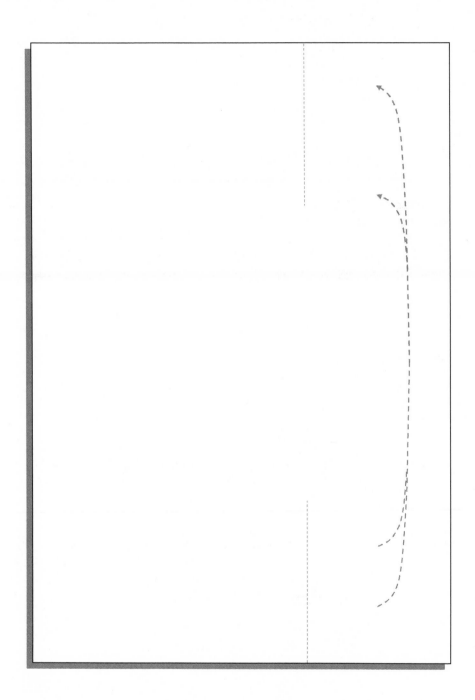

1.1 **According to 1 John 5:11-12, if someone has the Son (i.e. Jesus the Christ) what else do they have?**

1.2 **According to 1 John 5:11-12, if someone does not have the Son of God (i.e. Jesus the Christ) what else do they not have?**

2.0 **What happens at the very moment when someone believes with true biblical faith** (i.e. believes in Jesus, receives Jesus, has faith or trusts in Jesus, accepts Jesus, crosses over The Bridge, becomes regenerate, born again, saved, etc.)**?**

3.1 **The very essence or name of God is Trinitarian. God is _____ Persons yet only _____ true God.**

3.2 **Who are the three Persons of the one true God?**

4.0 **True** or **False. When someone becomes born again they become a new creation with the nature of their Heavenly Father; therefore, they will never sin anymore and life will be easy and they will be happy all the time.**

48

notes

Eternal life is a gift! The Bible says, "For by grace you have been saved through faith. And this is not your own doing; it is the gift of God, not a result of works, so that no one may boast."[66] Receiving eternal life is not based on what we have done, but rather on what God has done for us. God the Father has sent His Son. God the Son has sacrificially died on the cross and been raised the third day. God the Holy Spirit gives us new birth through faith in Jesus the Christ.

The gift of eternal life is something no one deserves and which no one can repay. There is nothing anyone can do to merit God's grace – it is a gift! Grace is God's unmerited favor given to man. It is a gift given through faith. Only those who have received the gift of eternal life through faith in Christ can serve God (i.e. good works). When we are given this new life, we have a relationship with the Father and can actually talk with Him (i.e. prayer). We are part of His family and bride (i.e. His church). We have been given a new nature – God's nature – and are immersed and identified with the one true God (i.e. spiritual baptism).

When we receive the gift of eternal life we are saved – saved from the deserved wrath of God. "For all have sinned"[67] and deserve, or have earned, eternal death.[68] "But God shows his love for us in that while we were still sinners, Christ died for us."[69] Someone has to pay the due penalty of sin to a just and holy God. We have one of two choices: either we can receive the penalty for our sin (this yields eternal death and damnation) or we can allow Christ to receive the penalty for our personal sin (this yields eternal life). The Bible says every knee will bow and tongue confess Jesus is Lord.[70] You can either do this now through faith and receive eternal life *or* you will do this after you physically die and experience the second death.

The following diagram illustrates the summary of this session:
- Write "**Ephesians 2:8-9**" under "John 1:12-13"
- Write "**Romans 3:23; 6:23; and 5:8**" under "Ephesians 2:8-9"
- Write your name and contact information on the bottom left

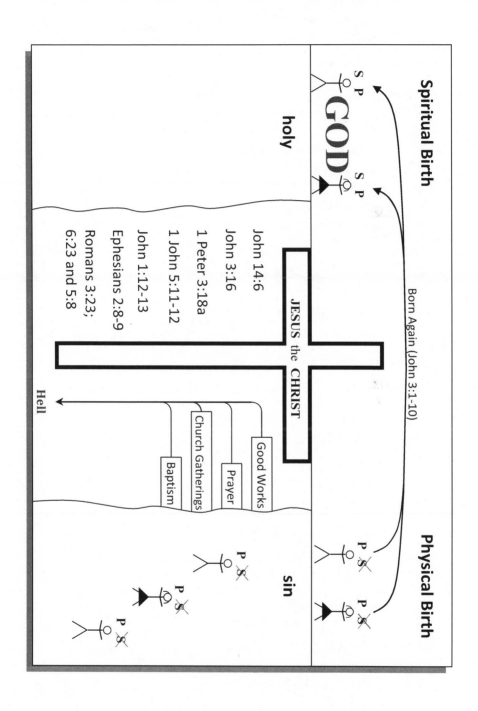

Session 7: *God's Speed*

Message	Drawing
Mankind's sole purpose is to glorify their Creator. If someone does not know Him they cannot fulfill their intended purpose. The only way to have a restored relationship with God is through faith in Jesus the Christ.	
"For by grace you have been saved through faith. And this is not your own doing; it is the gift of God, not a result of works, so that no one may boast."	Write "**Ephesians 2:8-9**" under "John 1:12-13"
"For all have sinned..." (Romans 3:23a)	Write "**Romans 3:23; 6:23; and 5:8**" under "Ephesians 2:8-9."
"For the wages of sin is death, but the free gift of God is eternal life in Christ Jesus our Lord." (Romans 6:23)	
"But God shows his love for us in that while we were still sinners, Christ died for us." (Romans 5:8)	

Now let's once again revisit the questions:
1). What should be the purpose and highest priority in one's life?
2). On a scale of 1-10 (ten being the highest) what is your desire to be living a 10 for God?

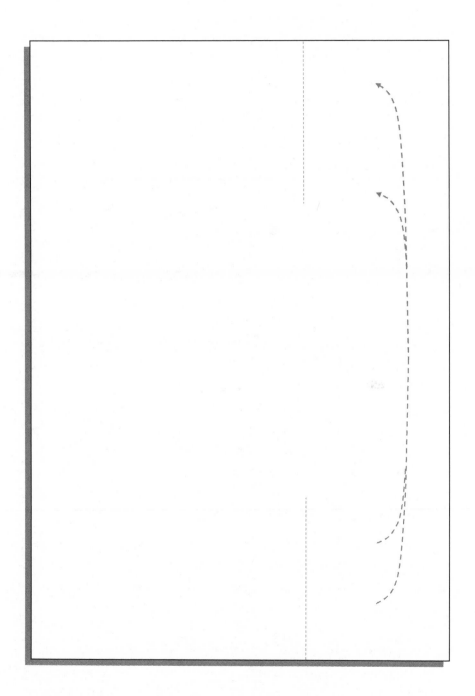

So what's next? If you have any interest in the previous sessions and have a desire to know God, then the simplest answer to the question, "What's next," is get to know God so you can fulfill the true purpose of your life. The only way to personally know God, is through His Son Jesus the Christ. But how does someone get to personally know Jesus? Today, the only way to personally know Christ is by knowing the truth about Him. The Holy Spirit personally reveals Jesus; and the only way He does this is through the truth of the Bible. In summary, the only way to fulfill the intended purpose of your life is knowing God by knowing Jesus as revealed through the truth of the Bible by the Holy Spirit.

How does someone learn how to properly interpret the Bible so they can get to know and glorify God? We have designed a discipleship curriculum to help with this very process. Through this curriculum, you will learn how to read and understand the Bible. You will be able to know the truth by developing the skills on how to study and properly interpret the Bible.   By developing the skills on how to study the Bible, along with the proper method of interpreting the Bible, the student will be able to properly interpret and understand the Truth of the Scriptures. As the student of the Bible interacts with the Truth, the Holy Spirit will transform the individual through their personal relationship with Jesus Christ. If you would like more information on these materials, simply ask the person who shared this "FAQ of the Christian Life" with you.

We are all at one spiritual place or another as we travel through this temporal journey here on earth. As I have said, I am just one beggar telling another beggar where I found bread. If you can help me find some more bread, I would be appreciative. If there is anything I could do to help you on your spiritual journey, I would be honored (email: randall.arthur@usa.com). No matter what your personal goals in life, they must be built upon the foundation of knowing your Creator in order to fulfill your intended purpose. God's speed as you travel on your spiritual journey to the everlasting!

1.0 **What is God's grace?**

2.0 **Look up in the Bible and write out the verse Romans 3:23.**

3.0 **Look up in the Bible and write out the verse Romans 6:23.**

4.0 **Look up in the Bible and write out the verse Romans 5:8.**

5.0 **How many people will bow down and confess that Jesus is Lord (Philippians 2:10-11)?**

6.0 **As we conclude the FAQ of the Christian faith, let's revisit the following two questions: 1). "What _should_ be the passion or purpose of your life? (i.e. why are you here...? how do you wish to be remembered...?) and 2). On a scale of one through ten (ten being the best), how are you doing in living this out?"**

Question #1:

Question #2: 1   2   3   4   5   6   7   8   9   10

The Gospel

The Gospel

Message	Drawing
In the beginning there was, is, and always will be, a holy and just God.	*Draw a horizontal line about a third the way down. Write "**GOD**" above line on left. Write "**holy**" under line*
He created everything, including the first humans. God first created Adam with both physical life and spiritual life.	*Draw a man stick figure above line with "**P**" (physical) and "**S**" (spirit) above line on right*
God also created Adam's wife, Eve, with both physical and spiritual life.	*Draw a woman stick figure with "**P**" and "**S**" above*
God created mankind to have a personal relationship with God so they could serve and glorify Him.	*Draw lines and arrows to show God's purpose in creating mankind* 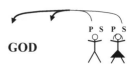
God instructed Adam, "You are free to eat from any tree in the garden; but you must not eat from the tree of the knowledge of good and evil, for when you eat of it you will surely die."	
Tragically, Satan successfully convinced Eve to eat the fruit from the tree of the knowledge of good and evil. After Eve ate the forbidden fruit she also gave some to her husband Adam, who was with her, and he also ate. When this happened, sin entered the world through Adam's act of disobeying God's Word.	*Write "**sin**" under the stick figures*

Message

When mankind disobeyed God's word, they immediately died spiritually; meaning, they became separated from God!

It was just as though a huge bottomless pit had opened between God and mankind's relationship. Mankind became sinful and therefore became separated from God. When Adam brought sin into the world by disobeying God's word, he inherited a sin nature; and in fact, mankind became enslaved by sin.

Adam and Eve lived what we might consider to be a 'normal' life. Adam and Eve physically lived to be very old and had many children, who had many children, and so on. All the people from Adam and Eve to you and me were physically born into this world with a nature to sin, which has been inherited from Adam from one generation to the next.

Since we all enter this world with the same sin nature as Adam, we also enter the world spiritually separated from God (i.e. spiritually dead) as a slave to sin.

Drawing

Place an "X" (spiritual death) through the "S" located above stick figures:

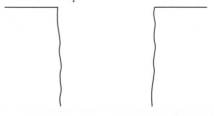

Open your paper as far as possible and draw the walls of the bottomless pit

Draw the additional stick figures under the other stick figures

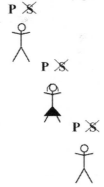

Write "P" above the additional stick figures (physical life)

Write "S" with an "X" through it above each additional stick figure (spiritual death)

Write "Physical Birth" in the top right hand corner of the paper

The Gospel

Message

Drawing

People often try and restore their relationship with God through their own efforts. We will call these human efforts "bridges."

One of the bridges people try to build is called "Good Works." People often believe if they do more good things than bad, then God will give us the benefit of the doubt and overlook our bad. This is not so.

"Prayer" is another bridge people often rely on to spiritually reunite them to God. Many people believe that they must sincerely ask God to forgive their sins or say some kind of prayer for their relationship with God to be restored. This is not so.

There are many people trusting in church membership and/or attending "Church Gatherings" to bridge the gap between God and man. This will never work.

For purposes of this illustration, the last bridge we will consider is the "Baptism" bridge. If one is relying on baptism to bridge their relationship with God, they are simply all wet.

Though all these bridges fall far short in bridging the gap between man and God, each of these so called bridges can have an important place in one's spiritual life.

Message

Drawing

As long as we are separated from God, our human devices and attempts to reach Him will be to no avail.

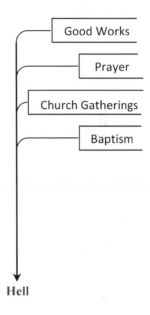

The tragedy is that when one's physical life on this earth comes to an end, and if they are still separated from God (i.e. spiritually dead) because of having trusted in erroneous ways of restoring their relationship with God, they will remain in that state forever. They will be separated from God forever in a place often referred to as hell (i.e. hades, the second death, lake of fire, etc.). The Bible calls this the second death because it is not the first death.

And do you know how the Bible describes spiritual death? The second death is the complete separation from God in total darkness and isolation, under perpetual judgment and torment, without hope, forever and ever and ever!   It is impossible for anyone to even begin to imagine how utterly horrible it is to be completely and permanently separated from God. Nor can words describe the misery that will be experienced by mind, soul, and body.

The Gospel

Message	Drawing
Jesus said, "I am the way, and the truth, and the life. No one comes to the Father except through me."	Write "**John 14:6**" on the left side of the chasm.
"For God so loved the world, that he gave his only Son, that whoever believes in him should not perish but have eternal life."	Write "**John 3:16**" under "John 14:6"
Jesus is the way, the truth, and the life. What did Jesus Christ actually do to become this bridge? By shedding His blood and dying upon the cross, being buried in the grave, and resurrected the third day according to the scriptures, Jesus became the life-giving savior that bridged the relational gap between all of mankind and God.	Draw the cross and write "**JESUS** the **CHRIST**" inside. 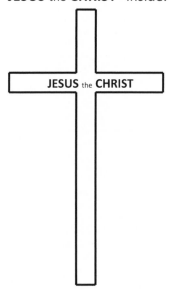
"For Christ also suffered once for sins, the righteous for the unrighteous, that he might bring us to God…"	Write "**1 Peter 3:18a**" under "John 3:16"

Message	**Drawing**
When we come to God by having faith in Jesus Christ, we pass from spiritual death to spiritual life.	Draw two new stick figures on the other side of the chasm, one on each side next to God. Write an "**S**" for spiritual life and a "**P**" for physical life above each stick figure.
To cross over from death to life, someone must receive Jesus and believe in His name. When someone has faith (i.e. trusts, believes, etc.) in Jesus they receive Him. To believe in His name is to believe in the very essence, the true complete identity, of His very being.	Draw an arrow from each stick figure on the "Physical Birth" side over to the "Spiritual Birth" side.
	Write "**Spiritual Birth**" in the upper left-hand corner.
"And this is the testimony, that God gave us eternal life, and this life is in his Son. Whoever has the Son has life; whoever does not have the Son of God does not have life."	Write "**1 John 5:11-12**" under "1 Peter 3:18a."
When we are born again, we become what the Bible calls a child of God. "But to all who did receive him, who believed in his name, he gave the right to become children of God, who were born, not of blood nor of the will of the flesh nor of the will of man, but of God."	Write "**Born Again (John 3:1-10)**" on top of the line connecting the stick figures.

Write "**John 1:12-13**" under "1 John 5:11-12." |

The Gospel

Message	Drawing
Mankind's sole purpose is to glorify their Creator. If someone does not know Him they cannot fulfill their intended purpose. The only way to have a restored relationship with God is through faith in Jesus the Christ.	
"For by grace you have been saved through faith. And this is not your own doing; it is the gift of God, not a result of works, so that no one may boast."	Write "**Ephesians 2:8-9**" under "John 1:12-13"
"For all have sinned…" (Romans 3:23a)	Write "**Romans 3:23; 6:23; and 5:8**" under "Ephesians 2:8-9."
"For the wages of sin is death, but the free gift of God is eternal life in Christ Jesus our Lord." (Romans 6:23)	
"But God shows his love for us in that while we were still sinners, Christ died for us." (Romans 5:8)	
Now let's once again revisit the questions: 1). What should be the purpose and highest priority in one's life? 2). On a scale of 1-10 (ten being the highest) what is your desire to be living a 10 for God?	

Scripture Footnotes

---

[1] John 14:21
[2] Matthew 7:15-20 with James 3:11-12
[3] Romans 3:23 with 5:12, 18-19
[4] Leviticus 11:44-45 with Hebrews 13:8 and Revelation 1:8
[5] Genesis 1
[6] Genesis 2:7
[7] Genesis 1:27
[8] Genesis 2:8
[9] Genesis 2:16-17
[10] Genesis 1:29-30; 2:10-11 with 2:15
[11] Genesis 2:20-22
[12] Genesis 3:2-3
[13] Genesis 3:6-7
[14] Romans 5:12
[15] Romans 8:3-17
[16] Genesis 3:7-8
[17] Romans 14:23
[18] Isaiah 14:12-15
[19] Luke 10:18
[20] Romans 5:12 with Romans 6:23
[21] Titus 1:2
[22] Matthew 10:28
[23] James 2:26
[24] Romans 6:19 with Genesis 6:5
[25] John 8:34 with Romans 6:19
[26] Genesis 3:23-24
[27] Genesis 3:17-18 with Romans 5:17
[28] Romans 5:12-21
[29] Isaiah 64:6
[30] 1 Samuel 16:7
[31] Romans 1:18-25
[32] John 3:36 with Revelation 20:10, 14-15
[33] 1 Timothy 2:3-4
[34] 1 John 4:8-10

[35] Psalm 14:1, 53:1
[36] John 14:6
[37] John 3:16
[38] John 8:32
[39] John 17:3
[40] John 10:10
[41] Matthew 1:23
[42] 1 Corinthians 15:2-4
[43] John 10:31
[44] Philippians 2:11
[45] Luke 18:27
[46] John 1:29
[47] Philippians 2:8-11
[48] Hebrews 4:15
[49] John 1:1, 14
[50] Luke 1:27, 34
[51] 1 Peter 3:18a
[52] Romans 5:7-8
[53] Romans 4:17
[54] 2 Corinthians 5:17
[55] John 1:6-7
[56] Matthew 4:17
[57] Ezekiel 36:26-27
[58] Luke 3:16
[59] Titus 3:5
[60] Deuteronomy 6:4
[61] Matthew 3:16-17
[62] John 17:4-6
[63] Matthew 28:16-20
[64] Matthew 28:19
[65] Romans 7:13-20
[66] Ephesians 2:8-9
[67] Romans 3:23
[68] Romans 6:23
[69] Romans 5:8
[70] Philippians 2:10-11

Made in the USA
Charleston, SC
10 February 2016